NEXT DOOR TO THE BUTCHER SHOP

ALSO BY RODNEY DeCROO:

Allegheny, BC

Next Door
to the
Butcher Shop

POEMS

Rodney DeCroo

 NIGHTWOOD EDITIONS

Nightwood Editions
P.O. Box 1779, Gibsons, BC, V0N 1V0
www.nightwoodeditions.com

Cover design by Angela Yen
Text design by Mary White
Printed and bound in Canada
This book has been produced on 100% post-consumer recycled, ancient-forest-free paper, processed chlorine-free and printed with vegetable-based dyes.

Nightwood Editions acknowledges the support of the Canada Council for the Arts, which last year invested $153 million to bring the arts to Canadians throughout the country. We also gratefully acknowledge financial support from the Government of Canada through the Canada Book Fund and from the Province of British Columbia through the BC Arts Council and the Book Publishing Tax Credit.

Cataloguing data available from Library and Archives Canada
ISBN 978-0-88971-330-7 (paper)
ISBN 978-0-88971-124-2 (ebook)

for Mark Thomas Evans

CONTENTS

III

I

CARGO SHIPS

This stinking tide swells under the moon's
pull. The gulls scream in the blackness beyond
the shore lights. The barnacled pillars

of the pier are the hoary legs
of a huge derelict Pan blowing a weedy flute.
Singer, your song dies in the damp sand

of this condom-strewn beach. Two drunken lovers,
huddled together, scuttle past crabwise,
pulling at each other, their laughter

echoing off the bathhouses. I am a hall
of echoes with many closed rooms. My friend,
your voice grows distant as I open door

after door searching for you, each opening
to this pier, this night, the bay and the faint lights
of the cargo ships travelling away.

IMAGINARY LANDMINES

I counted twelve feathers and attached each one
to the back of my hand. Some were black as the sap

of night's eternal tree. Others were white as the dove
thrown to the winds by the landlocked sailor

who rode the killing floods for a year and ten days.
For a moment my hand was an ostrich,

prehistoric and incapable of flight. A lizard's eye
flicked open like a switchblade and cut the light

that ran red as a ribbon swirled in a flushed toilet.
When my stomach exploded through my throat

I knew I'd hurt myself again. I didn't care.
I know you don't believe me, but a war

is a war though I'm not a soldier.
I'm an imaginary landmine that steps on itself.

BLACK COLUMNS

I could sleep for weeks in this bed, the black columns
of this room protecting me from the light. Indigent father
your ghost haunts the bus stations of Appalachia
seeking your cross-eyed war balladeer,
a toothless banjo resting on his hothouse knees.

The draft dodger, your brother, died thirteen times
in Canada, his ashes spread across Minnesota skies
like acid rain or grey tears returning to boyhood lakes
of eternal summer. He couldn't repair your fractured face
or make the greased stain of your M-16 disappear.

I live in a room in a terminal city. They pay me
because my head is broken. The relentless rain
striking the windows is the faint echo of gunshots
three generations ago through the fog of Europe.
I am your son. We have earned it like a wage.

PINK SUNS

Three days after she told me,
I went to Florida to visit my brother.
Or let me rephrase that: I went
there to get drunk on supermarket beer,

smoke cheap cigarettes, have drunken
fistfights over girls at the Freaky Teki Club
while they threw up in the bushes,

to get arrested outside the Piggly Wiggly
twenty-four-hour convenience store
at 2:30 a.m. for assaulting
a store clerk who called my brother

a hillbilly. My twenties, a blur of pain
and stupidity. She called my brother's place
early on a Tuesday morning.

My head ached from the night before.
I opened a beer and took the phone. She said
she'd had it done, didn't want to see me again.
I put the phone down and drank the beer

to calm my hands and my head.
The palm leaves outside the window clacked
loudly in the wind like the snapping beaks

of pelicans, crowding against my legs
the day before on the pier, their
empty maws flashing like pink suns.

MY FIRST GUITAR

The first guitar I ever played
was my mother's. I think I was four
or five years old. It sat in the corner
of the trailer's living room
covered with dust and without strings.

I imagined the sounds it made
as I dragged it into my bedroom
to perform secret concerts.

One night in a drunken argument
with my father, she smashed it
against the coffee table and snapped
the neck, a sickening sound

I never wished to repeat.
After that I avoided guitars,
looked away when I saw them,
afraid of what they'd say in my hands,
or worse, that I might break them.

OUTSIDE RACHEL'S HOUSE

On summer nights we play basketball
outside Rachel Sullivan's house. Her father
built the hoop for his daughters but it's us,
the neighbourhood boys, who use it. We play
horse, twenty-one and two-on-two as shadows
deepen and a handful of stars begin to twitch
above the street. Rachel and her friends sit
on the front porch steps to talk. They mock
us when we argue or strut our small victories
on the pavement. *Aw, grow up!* they shout,
rolling their eyes, their mouths full of laughter.
Wearing halter tops and shorts, their tanned bodies
glow in the slow humid dark, lighting our way
home long after Mrs. Sullivan yells that it is late,
goddamn it, and time for us to leave.

WE STEPPED RIGHT OVER THEM

For hours every day that summer
I banged bald tennis balls off the brick wall
of the Super Dollar Grocery. I used an old
Dunlop racket my mother had bought
at a yard sale for a couple dollars.
With paper route money I bought
vacuum-sealed cans of fuzzy balls
that I hit until they split or became so dead

they hardly bounced. John McEnroe
was my new hero. Throwing his racket
across the immaculate lawn of centre court,
shouting insults at the umpire in his raised chair,
giving the finger to the London press,
beating down with pounding serve and volley,
the graceful baseliner and five-time champion

the inscrutable Swede Björn Borg.
Odd hero for a welfare kid from a coal town
in western Pennsylvania—our own courts
used for street hockey and basketball,
made of black asphalt that stuck to your soles
in the sun. The metal nets dragged to the ground
by their heaviness, so bowed at the centre
we stepped right over them.

NEXT DOOR TO THE BUTCHER SHOP

Every Sunday night we'd scurry
like cockroaches from our basement suites
across the city to the Grind Café,

next door to the butcher shop at King Edward and Main,
to perform our poems and songs on the open stage.
There was thin, stooped and scowling David,

who quit university after reading *On the Road*,
bought a motorcycle for two hundred dollars
and drove it from Ontario to Vancouver

to live in a boarding house to write poems
about dead birds and crucifixes like his hero Bukowski.
And burly Tim from the Maritimes with poems

about his aunties, his big shoulders curled
and hunched beneath the weight of rain-sodden
wool sweaters, muttering into his beard and stained briefcase,

marketing schemes of poetry as a television-music video-
game show, avalanches of confetti, cocaine and groupies
for the winners and obscurity for those who lost,

who claimed he got drunk in an Irish pub
with Seamus Heaney who wrote him letters of admiration
which he couldn't produce at our request,

who disappeared into a locked basement
and a cloud of pot smoke and rumours of sexual assault,
hurled buckets of paint against the walls and called it art

until his stern lawyer father flew to town to take him home.
And Wendy who had no home to return to, her body
pierced, branded and tattooed, a living canvas

for the pain she'd known as long as breathing,
her eyes blackened with thick mascara
as if she was watching you from the bottom

of a well, sang with wine purpled lips giggling songs
about perverted unicorns and bands of psychotic fairies
prowling fantastical forests to prey on lost children,

who married a junkie painter and disappeared
into small town Alberta to become a slow alcoholic
suicide, her own children abandoned to the system

she never escaped. And the self-appointed high priest
of folk music Rick the Prick, who started writing in the sixties,
never played past the open stages from where

he snarled his bitter songs, preached poverty
as purity, popularity as selling out, who collected
young disciples to mock and cajole until they

revolted, and yet, sometimes onstage
such stripped and shining spaces between his words
and notes you almost believed him. And myself,

body tensed with anger, strutting leather-clad, chain-smoking,
would-be prophet of the working classes,
apocalyptic doomsayer, portrait of the young man

as an arrogant ass, shouting my poems at the small group
of faces gathered each Sunday night at the Grind Café,
next door to the butcher shop at King Edward and Main.

THE GOLDEN BIRD

I saw him behind the tavern at Union
and Pine. He was sitting on the steps
of the back door where the drunks
pissed at night. The IRON CITY BREW

sign light enough to see the belt
wrapped around his naked arm,
and the needle's lighting flicker
striking the dark branch of his vein.

I ducked behind Jimmy Shevchenko's
older brother's black Trans Am,
and with my hands on the front tire,
lifted my head and peeked

over the hood with its huge decal
of a fiery bird. His arm lay limp
along his thigh, the loosened belt
dangled at his elbow and the syringe

lay between his scuffed sneakers.
He dropped his head back, eyes
shut, and sat with his mouth agape.
The dark O shaped by his lips,

was the blackness of the hood
I hid behind. I lifted my hand
to touch the golden bird,
rising from the fire of the steel.

IN A VIOLENT TIME

I tried to tell you how it came at me
without warning, how it hung
in the stricken air about my face
all claws, piercing eyes and tearing beak.
How light streamed between the buildings
like a flash flood tearing trees from earth,
washing soil and roots away
with the force of a Gulliver
swatting down the Lilliputian years.
I tried to say but you were standing
on the street outside the clinic
on the year I was born, the black dust
of early morning Pittsburgh winter
gathering invisibly in your young hair
and eyes, the blackness passed to me
in the milk that gave me suck,
the tangled roots of iron and barges
heaped on the coal-strewn shores
of three filthy rivers in the mighty labour
of a land not even your father
could find a prayer to satisfy.
How it came to me like a blast
of wind from the angel's furnace mouth,
ripping my voice in two,
the curtain torn, the darkened sky,
the silence before the unrequested song,
that in your ignorance and unyielding love
was what you gave me.

ONLY THE LIGHT

I am running faster than ever before.
My body is capable of anything.
My feet scarcely touch the ground

and when they do they leave no marks.
Do not look for me in the usual places.
You will not find me in the apartment
among cat hair and dust, nor in the produce

markets with their inventories of perfectly
shaped and tasteless fruit, nor in cafés
with those who do not speak to me or I
to them, nor in the streets with brawling drunks
or sullen faces anticipating rain and months

of darkness. My arms and legs pump
effortlessly. I am beginning to disappear,
my skin glows from so much heat.
It is painless, a purification. I did not think
it possible. Soon, there will be nothing left;
only the light will remain.

SYLVIA

You wrote everything blue,
a slow-motion asphyxiation
sounded out in syllables,
an umbilical cord wrapped
around a globe, an alabaster
neck going cold. I saw your
saints floating in a row, eyes
shut like night flowers against
a lunar glow, ghastly as the
reflected light only a murder knows.

Oh statue, what ball of snakes,
what unbending stare brought
you to this, this rigidity of flight,
this perfect arrow into dawn?

THE DEBT

By day I stole jeans from department stores
in Thunder Bay and sold them at night
in a booze can with my friend Wayne. We
sat drinking from stubby brown bottles
of High Test, the jeans piled on a chair
next to me bristling with price tags.
Wayne was a large Ojibwa man who used
his size to intimidate customers when they
tried to haggle. He'd stand up to look down
on them. *Pay him what he wants or fuck off.*

The stranger would stammer an apology
and give me the cash. After they left
we lowered our heads to hide our smiles.
Wayne owned a hair salon and spent his days
giving perms to old ladies who came
to tease and gossip with him. His mother
had been a barmaid and he grew up in the bars
of the oil patch and logging towns and knew
the ways of violence. Wayne and I met outside
his salon as I sold cigarettes on the street.

He bought the entire carton of Player's Lights
and offered to take me to lunch. I knew
what he wanted by the way he placed his money
in my palm. I'd been approached by men
before but I was hungry and it was winter
so I went with him. We spent the day and deep
into the night drinking at a bar filled with old
men who sat alone with sleeves of pale draft
beer tasting like vomit and piss. We left
after last call staggering over icy sidewalks

and falling into parked cars, the moisture
of our breath freezing against our faces, the ache
of coldness pulsing through my finger-bones
and wrists to pierce my drunkenness.
I had to find a place to stay the night. Wayne
beckoned me to follow. I walked head-down,
crushing ice and snow beneath my boots
until we came to houses separated by vacant lots
along the lake. Wayne pulled a portion of chain
link fence high enough to scramble beneath.

We crossed under the opposite fence and into
the backyard of a brick house the colour of dried
blood. The windows blackened out with newspaper
and tin foil. The only light, a bulb above the basement
door. Wayne lurched down the steps steadying himself
against the concrete stairwell and banged the door.
As we waited, I felt the silence swirling around us
coming in from the huge night over the frozen wastes
of Lake Superior, the freezing wind as hard
and unforgiving as iron or steel. Light rushed out

through the open door to reveal a woman: black
hair streaked with grey. Her face thin with narrow
eyes that cut like the neat, sharp teeth of a fox.
I followed Wayne and the woman into the acrid
warmth of the smoke-filled, weakly lit basement:
a wide room with a concrete floor and oil cloth
card tables between metal poles bearing the full
weight of the house. I could see the hunched shapes,
people in groups of twos or threes around the tables.
In the back, the woman sat by a yellow refrigerator

filled with bottles of beer. Next to her a space heater
glowed and rattled like an angry coiled snake, a stench
like burnt plastic. Wayne and I sat and drank. Cigarettes
burned in the alcoholic gloaming like the red eyes
of demons. For four months of my twentieth year
I sold stolen clothing, stumbling with Wayne through
desolate winter dawns to pass out on his couch where
I fended off his drunken tearful gropes. Locking
myself in the bathroom as he punched the door
cursing me for failing to pay what he was owed.

WHY IS YOUR POETRY SO DARK?

I wanted to sit down in the sidewalk and bite people's legs,
I wanted to take this blackness inside and throw it everywhere
like paint onto everything until the world looked the way I felt,
I wanted to rip out my veins and braid them into a noose
to hang myself from a street lamp like a psychotic Christmas
ornament, I wanted to dig up my father's bones and tell each one
I hated him, I wanted to leap from my skull like a man trapped inside
a burning skyscraper, I wanted to time travel to my sixteen-year-old
mother and give her a condom, I wanted to punch my own face bloody
and bruised, which I did, until I passed out and told people
I'd been jumped by my eternal nemesis. I wanted to get so high
the silence was louder than the pain, I wanted to fuck my way back
to the nothingness I came from, I wanted to burn God's face off
with a flamethrower then douse him with a thimble of water,
I wanted to become a herd of horses and stampede into a forest fire.

PASSING THROUGH

Ten minutes after midnight. I've just finished
dinner: chicken, black bean sauce and rice.
Outside the wet streets gleam beneath
the curved necks of street lamps bending over
them like angels of wood, light and steel.
Eight years ago I dragged myself
through a Montreal winter like a sack
of ashes, my hands cramped, frozen
and red, saying a name again and again
that was my own. I hurt myself
into the moment desperate to be truly alive.
Like a drowning man breaking
the surface gulping air until the lungs
nearly burst. The rent is paid,
the cat sleeps in my lap and there is
two days' worth of food in the fridge.
Tomorrow I'll try to write poems
and walk by the docks, to trace
my shadow beneath the mountains
above the churning, wind-tossed bay—
to pass through so much, to need so little.

THE CHAIR

From the night alley
the bottle collector's cart
rattles like a shaken cage
as he pushes it over the potholed
asphalt. What is he looking for,
rummaging his hands through
the night's guts? A liver, a kidney,
a lung, a deformed and oversized heart
to lug around like a pot roast
among his rags and bottles?
From my bed in midnight's room,
I see only darkness in the chair.
But he is there. His breath rasps
like a cage door, opening.

FUNERALS, DISASTERS AND WEDDINGS

I stand inside this old room like a traveller
stranded at an airport besieged by winter.
A transistor radio with a broken tuning dial
lies in the corner, a torn grey sheet
hangs in the open window the weather

pours through, a creased magazine
page of Christ's face is taped to the wall
watching me with blackened eyes.
My breath gives shape to a ghost.
Nothing has changed. It was always cold.

I touch the blue passport inside my jacket.
It confirms my citizenship elsewhere.
I no longer belong to this place,
but like funerals, disasters and weddings,
I am sometimes required to return.

THE COST OF LEAVING OR SONG OF THE SUICIDE

The cost of leaving is a swarm of beaks and feathers
        as you run a wind tunnel that doesn't end.
The cost of leaving is a small fire in the marrow
        of your bones, consuming you from the inside out.
The cost of leaving is a blind child juggling knives.
The cost of leaving is waking alone with a side
        aching like Adam.
The cost of leaving is a Christ lost in a forest of crucifixes.
The cost of leaving is an ocean of oil drowning the world.
The cost of leaving is a minotaur in every room
        where all doors lock behind you.
The cost of leaving is throat torn shards
        of powdered glass when you sing.
The cost of leaving is a face of tar and splintered wood
        eclipsing all the moon's faces.
The cost of leaving is the unopened letter pinned
        to your chest.
The cost of leaving is a guitar with a snapped neck.
The cost of leaving is the moment in a coal mine
        before it explodes.
The cost of leaving is the constant darkness behind
        your right ear.
The cost of leaving is the endless silence of white walls.
The cost of leaving is the scream buried in the carpet.
The cost of leaving is the broken backs of snails
        and irises of frost.
The cost of leaving is a crowd of jaundiced stares.
The cost of leaving is less than the cost of staying here.

II

THE ECLIPSE

Three days before the solar eclipse
my mother warned me not to look.
The light would burn my retinas,
turning sight to blindness. Afraid I
couldn't resist the urge to stare,
I planned to hide in my room
on the day of the darkling sun.
The night before, my father stood
beside my bed and made a fist,
a bony moon, slid it by the ceiling
bulb until it blocked the light. *That's
all it is,* he said. *There's no magic.
It can't hurt you, now go to sleep.*
He hit the switch, shut the door
and the room went black.

GONE

My first apartment was a basement suite
near 41st and Oak. The owner, Craig,
a former drug dealer turned contractor
after a five-year stint in Oakalla,
rented to young people down on their luck.
I found the place through an ad
in the Social Assistance office.
The interview was in his kitchen.
C'mon, he said, *have something to eat!*

I was hungry. I hadn't eaten for two days
after spending my money getting drunk
at the Cobalt. *Listen*, he said, *you're
not leaving this kitchen until you've had
one of Diane's sandwiches. There you go!*
he shouted, smacking the table.
Are you looking for work? Yes, I said.
*I'm looking for labourers. You want to work
for me?* Again, the smack on the table.

As I ate the thick bread and rich meat
and drank the dark coffee offered to me,
I knew the hunger in my stomach,
my unwashed clothes and my trembling hands
as if for the first time. After he left me
in the furnished suite, I stood with my back
against the door looking at the room.
I wondered who'd been here before me
and why they were gone.

THE VISITOR

The rain striking the aluminum siding
is the irregular tapping of Morse code:
the night relaying a message
but to whom I don't know. Nor can I

decipher pauses and taps
into meaning; an archaic art
left to Boy Scouts and hobbyists,
and has turned me dumb and deaf.

Eyes shut I surrender to the rain's
inconstant but unceasing rhythm,
a piano of watery darkness
dissolves my thoughts to sleep.

And now transparent as water
you come, a small tornado of smoke
twisting over your glassy shoulder,
your blue dangling feet

inches above the gravel path,
hanging in the air, half ghost,
half bird of prey, you watch me,
eyes sharp as a beak or talon.

When you died you kept dying in me,
until your name became the same
as the death behind my breath,
each time I raised my voice to sing.

DENNY

His hair was oiled and slicked
back. He drove a blue sixty-eight Camaro
with white racing stripes and worked
at the steel mill. My mother said he
didn't drink much, was a Vietnam
vet like my father. Denny moved
into the apartment next door to us.
There were rumours he'd beaten his ex-fiancée,
a girl from New Kensington. My mother
knew Denny since high school, remembered
him as the silent kid alone in the cafeteria,
who didn't go to parties or play football.
Denny had a large eight-track collection
and played the Who, Cream and Zeppelin
so loud my mother banged the wall,
shouted at him to turn the music down.
One Saturday night my mother found
him sitting outside his apartment so drunk
he couldn't stand. When he raised his head
his eyes were raw from crying. She
sat with him for hours reading aloud
from the new testament, testifying
that Christ had saved her life.

That Sunday Denny came to church
with us. His eyes were still red,
he reeked of too much aftershave,
and his large hands trembled. *So much
for doesn't drink much*, my brother
whispered as we followed our mother
and Denny up Colfax Street. I sat next

to Denny in the pew, mother on the other
side. He was sweating and kept pulling
at his collar to loosen his tie. He took off
his suit-jacket and hung it over the back
of the pew, dark blooms of sweat beneath
his arms. When the collection came around,
Denny stood, pulled a handful of change
from his pocket and dumped it into the plate,
half the coins spilling loudly onto the floor.
He bent between the pews as people
stared, my mother stiff as the granite columns
framing the entrance to the church.

Denny stood with the rest of us, looking
down at the closed hymnal in his hands.
My mother leaned close, holding her opened
book in front of him. He shifted his eyes
to the black print and he spoke out loud,
The Lord is my redeemer, he shall lift me up,
then began to laugh, his eyes clenched shut,
his entire body shaking. The singing
stopped as parishioners turned to watch.
When my mother touched his shoulder
his head snapped up and his eyes opened.
Don't touch me, he said, and pushed past me,
knocking me into the pew. I watched his rigid
back as he walked between the rows of sullen
faces, toward the huge white doors
and what waited outside for him.

REACHING BEDROCK

While clearing stones caught
in the metal grid of the sluice box
I found our first nugget. Half the size
of my thumb, it glinted dull yellow
through its dirt coat. I grabbed it
and ran to the camp. My father
was chopping wood. He turned,
the axe dangling at his side. I held
out my fist before him. Slowly
I opened it palm up, like a magician

revealing the object of his trick.
He stared at the dirty lump of gold.
Behind him shreds of morning mist
slid over the tangled clear-cut
stretching the hill to Spectacle Lake.
He dropped the axe and stepped
toward the creek. *Come on, we must
be close to bedrock*, he said.
What about this? I held the nugget
out to him. *Put it in the truck,*

somewhere safe. I climbed into the cab
and pulled out the ashtray packed
with stubbed ends of Marlboro cigarettes
and empty brass casings of .22 shells.
I closed it and popped open the glove
compartment. Inside was a mickey
of Jack Daniel's resting on an oil-stained
road map of Western Canada.

I slipped the nugget into my pocket
and reached for the whiskey. I twisted

the black cap to crack the seal
and held it up to swallow, wincing
at the burn in my throat and guts.
I drank until the mickey was nearly
empty. I put the cap back and tossed
the bottle to the floorboards. I exhaled
hard to keep the contents down. I laid
on the soft bench of the cab, the vinyl
cool against my face. From the creek,
I heard my father shouting my name.

CLEAR-CUT

I move slowly across the clear-cut,
between boulders, fallen trees and torn-up
mounds of earth. The sky glowers down
upon me, medieval throwback, witch burner,
so blue it has mistaken itself for eyes.
Father, I feel you watching from the treeline
above, your hard face hidden among branches.
Have you crossed your crossed sights
across my stupid heart? I feel something
catching at my ribs. I know what it is.

Your decision weighed in a scarred and crooked
finger. I stop and count my breaths, concealed
behind a tumble of dropped poplars,
their pulp useless like my potted words
that refuse to grow a different face, a clumsy
grace you can't show. Soon night will descend
like an eye punched shut. We'll inhabit
this wilderness together, you asleep among
the ancient trees, myself bundled into the
scooped-out earth that fits me like a grave.

THE DEER

My friends and I dragged the gutted carcass
of the deer through a field of snow towards
the truck. Tufts of brown hair and smeared
streaks of blood marked the path made
by the slack body. The rope around the long
neck twisted the head unnaturally, a dead black
eye staring up at us. I was a sixteen-year-old
boy in western Pennsylvania. Sure, I'd shot
grouse and rabbits, caught and clubbed
trout to death, had slit the throats of geese
on my uncle's farm, but when I placed
the black sight upon the deer's heart
it looked back at me as if to give itself
to my need to make a death, robbing me
of the cold power I sought in my killing.

MY FATHER'S BEARD

My father's beard is not a river though many men
      have drowned in it.
My father's beard grows in the grave pushing through earth
      like the blind snouts of moles.
My father's beard is the hangman's rope that snaps the neck.
My father's beard is blacker than the Black Forest and spans
      fourteen continents,
My father's beard is a lamp of tangled fireflies guiding travellers
      through the night. The streaks of grey in
my father's beard are tendrils of starlight threading ever-expanding
      space.
My father's beard is the tall grass where the wounded lion
      crouches as it waits for the hunter.
My father's beard restored Samson's strength and brought down
      his enemies.
My father's beard is a web of fibre optics transmitting data to millions
      of devices, to billions of minds.
My father's beard is the bow and the strings and the song
      brought forth.
My father's beard troubles the dreams of physicists.
My father's beard is the nuclear cloud burning the sky's face.
My father's beard is a field of darkness full of snares and I am
      a small animal that dares not move.

THE PIER

On a Florida night that clings
to the skin like a warm wet towel
we walk onto the long pier.
The dock lamps cast gold light
that fails to show the black waters
slapping the pillars below us.
I carry a bait bucket filled with earth
and night crawlers, a red cooler
with our sandwiches and drinks.
My grandpa carries our fishing poles
and the dented tackle box
he'd bought for me eighteen years ago
on my fifteenth birthday. He stops
to talk to an older man who leans
against the railing watching his line
disappear into the darkness below.
How's the fishing tonight? asks Grandpa.
The man turns to us with a slow smile.
No bites, but it's peaceful.
I wonder at the easy friendliness
these strangers greet each other with,
me always tense with men my age.
I step forward and shake the man's hand.
It's hard and calloused like Grandpa's.

HUCK IN CASCADIA

In the campfire's twitching light
I sit on a stump reading *Huckleberry
Finn*. Huck's talking about the raft
at night, the sky speckled with stars

and how Jim claims the moon
laid them like a frog lays eggs.
I lower the book and look up
at the small patch of sky

ringed by the jagged tops
of black pines, thick with stars,
like a swirl of snowflakes
suspended in space.

A snorted breath, like a man
clearing his throat, and there,
just beyond the fragile globe
of light a patch of denser black

within the blackness;
a set of eyes reflecting fire,
a black bear on its haunches
watching me. That evening

I'd hiked in on a logging road
two miles off the highway,
to find this spot beyond the sound
of passing trucks and cars.

Now, the Similkameen River
is the roar of nameless water
charging through the dark forest.
I touch the book and wait.

THE WEATHER KEEPER

The weather keeper has watery eyes
two slick, sad, sanctimonious white balls
scanning nothing, black pupils deep as coal mines.
I've beaten her appetites back again and again,
scarred but not scared by her nervy lightning.
Over jagged rooftops her maw opens to the sun.
She scolds my obsession with mirrors, dull delusions.
I wake to the green stink of rainforests, her hair
matted against my windows. I'm trapped by roots
white as the undersides of her wrists.

ULTRASOUND

I almost died of pneumonia at twenty-three,
trying to hack up the clawed thing in my lungs.

My forehead burned like a hot plate. From the mattress
on the floor in a damp basement, I saw Sylvia Plath's

face in an imaginary tulip that was the mane of a horse
I couldn't ride. I tried to kill myself with sleep.

They put me in a room and locked me in at night
until I remembered how to dissemble. I still

think of you, your ghost like a small black comma
at the centre of a storm we couldn't hold.

APPLES
     for Milton M.

It was snowing in Vancouver the day
you died. I was repainting my apartment,
covering Mediterranean blue walls
with layers of eggshell white.
I was determined to work through the day
and into the night until the job
was done. I'd stopped to make lunch
when the phone rang. *You need to go*
see Milton, Rodney. Ruby says he's only
got another day. Maybe two.

I showered, scrubbing paint from my skin
and hair. I ironed my clothes and dressed.
At the door I looked back into the apartment:
the furniture and carpet were covered by white
sheets, as if the falling snow had fallen
inside the walls. The blue paint dark beneath
the first coat of white was flowing water under ice
too thin to walk on. I took the residential streets
to the hospital. The black branches of the giant,
leafless oaks arched above me like the charred
roof of a burnt-out cathedral. I listened
to the silence of the snowed-in streets
as I walked to find some calm. The hallway

to your room was wide, the bleached white floor
shined like the full moon's gaunt face on a winter's
night. The smell of human waste rose from canvas
hampers filled with soiled bedding and gowns.
Empty wheelchairs sagged askew by walls.

I passed quiet rooms, the patients hidden
in their beds behind beige curtains. I entered
your room and sat by your bed to watch you sleep.
It was as if someone had left a shrunken mask
of the face I knew lying on the pillow. I held
your hand. It was cold as the snow falling
on the city. A nurse came in and pulled a narrow

table across your bed: a tray and cutlery.
Would you like to feed him? He likes
the applesauce, said the nurse as she took
the cart and pushed it from the room.
You tried to lift your head from the bed,
but fell back on the pillow. Your hands grasped
the railings, but still you were too weak
to lift yourself. You kept saying: *No,*
I won't. No, no, I won't. I leaned my face
in front of yours. Your eyes found me
and you grinned. I picked up a spoon and dipped
it in the applesauce and moved it to your mouth.

You closed your lips around it and swallowed.
Those apples are good! Your eyes shined
like polished fruit as the boy took your voice.
I fed you several times and after each
you asked for more until you shut your eyes.
I stayed another hour, holding your hand
as you slept. When I first got sober you'd
drop me off at the small room I called home,
saying before I left your car, *You're alright*
babe. You just don't know it yet.

THE OTHER MOUTH

Green and patient, the plant
creeps imperceptibly across the white windowsill.

Oh hothouse, what dreams
grow in your clouds of stifling warmth?

The cat stares from its perch
atop the bookshelf sagging with words, words, words.

It doesn't trust the yellow guitar in the corner;
yellow mouth of the moon before an eclipse.

And that other mouth, the oven's dark stage,
blackened by the burnt offerings of the god

in the machine and his desperate contrivances.
It will take years to scrub it clean.

CATCH AND BURN

Under the dirt is all the darkness
you want and silence too. I speak
the words as I sit on the edge of my bed.
I stare at the white columns of my legs
consumed by a fire that doesn't burn,
flame-shadows thrashing the walls.
The pain should be unbearable,
but I've learned to say the words
the fire brings and for my tongue
I'm spared. In the flames I see a crow
pecking at the burst guts of a squirrel
crushed by a car. The squirrel's eyes
are black as the eyes of the feeding crow,
as my eyes are the darkness that watches
the burning shapes. I say the words *squirrel,
crow, blackness, eyes* into the emptiness
of the room. The fire grows each time
I speak. When I've said all the words,
these walls will catch and burn.

III

THE CITY OF LIGHT

I'd tear down all of it with my own hands,
I'd drench this apartment in gasoline
and toss the flared match to walk away
and never stop until my abandoned life
became an inferno against the city's night sky.

I'd stand for days along the edges of expressways
to sing off-key into the screams of semi-trailers
and cars until I stood within a cocoon of silence

and flashing shadows. I'd enter every gas station,
truck stop and roadside bar to ask each face
their chosen name, until I heard the name behind
each name, and saw the tiny flame in the caves
of their mouths. I'd carry bags of crushed potato chips

to feed the crows until they croaked a blessing
and forgiveness upon me. I'd kneel in rest areas
and tourist centres to repent of every good deed
I'd ever done, until I met the god within my crimes,
bearing directions back to the City of Light.

THE SHEET

I told you to take everything but the futon,
the small kitchen table and a chair.

My movements echoed in the bare rooms
when I came home from work that evening.

You left a note on the table and one sheet
on the futon. I was angry you'd taken

both pillows and all the blankets. I sat
on the chair and opened the folded note.

It was a list of my faults and your hope
that I would get the help I needed.

I ripped the page into small pieces
and flushed them down the toilet.

I went to the bedroom and tore
the sheet off the futon, pushed it through

the window to let it lie on the sidewalk below.
It's tangled shape seemed a prostrate body.

I laid on the hardwood floor next to where
we'd slept each night. When I awoke,

the apartment was dark. Someone was knocking
at the front door. With outstretched arms, I shuffled

through blackness until my hand found the knob
and turned. You were standing in the grainy light

of the hallway. You had the sheet in your hands.
Take it, you said. *It's yours.*

THE MANAGER AT THE SANTA BARBARA DELI

The manager at the Santa Barbara Deli
thinks I'm a shoplifter. She follows me
aisle to aisle as I look for items on my list.
She watches my hands as I gently squeeze
the peaches, hold up a can of soup to read
its ingredients. She knows I've concealed
beef bouillon and baby carrots under my long
greasy hair, that my unruly beard is stuffed
with cans of tuna, my pockets loaded
with soft drinks and chocolate bars. I worry
about the manager at the Santa Barbara Deli.

She has black rings beneath her eyes
because of my imaginary crimes. She's done
the inventory and knows I've taken the three
missing cartons of Greek yogourt
and two unaccounted-for frozen pizzas.
The manager at the Santa Barbara Deli
is getting thinner. She's become too anxious
to eat. She knows I'm a sexual deviant
plotting to steal more than the produce
she so lovingly displays for maximum freshness.

The manager at the Santa Barbara Deli
is concerned about my political views.
She knows I'm a terrorist, has visions of me
assembling bombs by candlelight to blow
up the delicatessen and the adjoining dairy
section. The manager at the Santa Barbara Deli
has heard that I'm a writer of poetry and songs.
She has no use for useless things. She knows

the increasing rates of shrinkage will bankrupt
the Santa Barbara Deli and she will default
on payments for a house she can't afford.

She will become homeless and forced to sleep
in the needle and condom-strewn alleys
and doorways of the Downtown Eastside.
Therefore she has instructed the stock boys
to apprehend me the next time I come into
the Santa Barbara Deli. They will take me
to a concrete room at the back of the store
containing only a chair and a steel desk
where she will interrogate me until with tears
streaking my face, I confess that I'm
the manager of the Santa Barbara Deli.

WINTER RUSHES IN

The window is broken. I swatted
the hissing, black speck of a fly with
a rolled magazine and smashed the glass.
The winter rushes in. My bloodless skin
goes white as your Munich snow
beneath the electric pallor of midnight's
fluorescent light and the lone walker's
long Antarctic stare. You're everywhere,
each atom in the air whispers of distances
farther than the mind no man fathomed.
The freeze must come as the sun, undone
by its own fires, fades so my brief heart
consumes itself upon these floors
like a struck pig in the slaughterhouse
blood flood. The tenants can't be told,
the shattered pane can't be fixed.

WAKE

I saw you leaving the clinic with the bandage wrap
you'd stolen bulging from your jacket's side pocket
like a pregnant belly: a mythic baby due to erupt
from your side or maybe a proletarian Eve

her naked skin aglow with afterbirth or the tears
of a distressed and minor god. I watched you
waiting at the bus stop, clenching and unclenching fists,
two hard, slow-motion hearts. Did you think your illness

was a secret? I couldn't feel the hooks of your malaise
pulling at my skin as you passed. We paddled a yellow canoe
along the edges of a weedy lake, grinning adventurers
among the stinking lily pads you chopped with every stroke.

You warned against the boggy waters; sedgy depths
millennia deep. *Who knows what's buried there?* you said,
watching the watery vortex dug by your paddle spin away,
clouds of airy stars streaming through our wake.

HALFWAY LIGHT

Above the rooftops I see silhouettes
of the North Shore mountains
and the flashing tips of the orange cranes
loading and unloading cargo ships
along the waterfront.

I've lived in Vancouver for twenty-eight
years and still don't call it home. Home
is a place I haven't seen since the day
I left. A sixteen-year-old boy
as determined as I'd ever be

climbing on a bus. This evening light
is a halfway light I wait for each day.
Like the light over the wide muddy fields
and farmhouses of Ohio as I sat on a bus
imagining a city of mountains.

The old man next to me croaking for air,
his huge fingers fumbling to hold a plastic
inhaler to his lips to clear his lungs.
I'm forty-six now and that old man
must be dead, his work-scarred hands

and labouring lungs dissolved to dust.
I think of him as I stand at the corner
of Hastings and Commercial watching night
fill the sky above the cranes, and the mountains
gone black as the hanging clouds.

How we rode beside each other for sixteen
hours and not once did he speak to me.
I remember turning to catch his profile
in the flux of thinning light and shadow:
the shut eye and the twitching ball

beneath the lid, the grey skin pitted and tight
across the bones of the face, how against the flicker
of fields it became a visage of shale and slate,
a travelling stone—thrown west.

WHY I HATE FLOWERS

I'm so fucking sick of flower poems.
I want to pull every single flower
poem up by their pungent flowery heads
and drag them, their dirt-clogged roots
hanging behind me, and throw them
in the dumpster out back. Fuck you
and your ponderous catalogues of Latin
names. Yeah, yeah I know, flowers
are God's handiwork. Well, so
are explosions, car crashes, fistfights,
mould and class war. When I was a kid,
flowers meant someone was dead.
Otherwise, who could afford the expense?

WHY CAN'T YOU BE LEONARD COHEN?

She told me she disliked my poems,
that poetry should be beautiful, stylish,
sad and romantic. She said Leonard Cohen
was her ideal of a poet and a lover.
She spent a week in Montreal
wandering the streets, reading his books
in cafés, listening to his songs at night
in her hotel room. She said I was just
a dry drunk with anger issues
and a penchant for making
everyone around me miserable.
And why couldn't I be handsome?
Leonard Cohen was handsome in his way.
He tried, but you, you're just ugly.
Like your poems and your songs,
just ugly and mean. And why,
why couldn't I see the beauty in the world?
I told her that her assessment
of my poetry and songs was probably
the most accurate I'd heard.
But she was wrong on one point.
I'd seen the beauty of this world and known
it was not meant for people like us.

TWO CITIES

Through a bus window
dotted with clinging drops of rain,
I watch as yesterday's snow
turns to grey slush. I'm headed downtown
for a collection of poetry by Gerald Stern,
a ninety-one-year-old Jewish-American
from Pittsburgh, the city of my youth.

I want to read again, on the printed page,
the poem about the feral cat in Rome
that stole half his sandwich
and ate it beside him
as he waited for a last night
with a young married woman
he loved but never saw again.

I want to read about the love
given up and the life gained
and the twisted and cunning face
of the cat as it chewed.
I want to laugh, feeling more
like that thin cat gulping down
a stolen sandwich than I do Stern.

Sweating inside my winter jacket,
headed downtown through the sleet
and slush of December, wondering
what bargain I made, what sacrifice
I offered to the starving cat of fate
when the man seated in front of me turns
and speaks: "Don't be fooled by the weather,
the day is more beautiful than you think."

Then he stands up and gets off at the next stop.
I live in two cities, both never
what they seem to be and always,
always more beautiful.

THE SLIM SHAPES OF COYOTES

I sit on a bench at Trout Lake after midnight.
The street lamp shining through the black
branches of the trees is a moon seen through
the cracked lens of a telescope, a firefly caught
in a spider's web, its feeble light illuminating
the strands. Before me, the sleeping lake
is the glazed head of the black Buddha meditating
in the window of an antique shop on Main.
Croaking frogs are old men clearing their throats
in the early morning dark of a rooming house
in Thunder Bay. I'm forty-five now and lead
a quiet life. I no longer steal, drink or smoke.
I sit by an artificial lake at night to wait
for the slim shapes of coyotes through the trees.

McCLEAN'S CAFE

Wendel had a greasy spoon near Broadway
and Burrard. It was called McClean's
and the college kids lined up on weekends
to cure their hangovers with greasy food
and black coffee. The most popular item
was the breakfast special for $2.75:
your choice of sausages or bacon, hash browns,
eggs and toast. I worked the floor, taking
orders, serving meals, clearing tables
and seating new arrivals. Wendel kept
a bottle of bourbon hidden among the sacks
of potatoes in the kitchen for himself
and the staff. We were more hung over
than the kids we served. *Booze sick* was how
Diane the fifty-year-old waitress put it,
her hands trembling as she poured herself
a drink before we opened the doors.
Youssef the Egyptian cook would shake
his large, grey head as he pushed mounds
of sausages over the grill. *Why do you drink?*
he'd ask. *I don't drink. I'm not sick.*
I'm happy. Then he'd shake his head again
and start to sing. Diane would gulp back
her drink and watch Youssef, her eyes
as yellow as the fragile yolks he'd drop
from cracked eggs to fry on the hot steel.
Honey, she'd say, *I drink for the same reasons
you don't. So shut the fuck up and do your job.*

FIX

I'll drag you down, down, down into mud,
I'll clutch, grab, pull 'til hair rips skull. Now,
we're getting to it, now, we're getting close,
now the bone's ghost is showing in the tobacco
skeleton of my lungs' grief tree. See, I've not
forgotten how to choke! See, I've not forgotten
how to stop breath in a bitten fist! See, I've not
forgotten the scooped out hallowed husk of a prayer
in the back of a plywood closet! Each forgiveness
is a light shoved in the face of darkness
until something burns, each blood drop is a psalm
that's tasted knife, each freedom is a larger cell
than the one before. I crave light like a junkie
wants junk. I'll even steal your bones to fix it.

SHARPENED PRICKS OF NOTHING

You sharpen the sky with your fingers
to a point. A point of nothing, a point beyond
even the pin-prick stars sparkling the backside
of our brains, a spatter of shotgun pellets.
It's all blood and meat in your butcher-shop
heart but you fling pails of bleach around
your chambers like alcoholics pour lies between
each drink. The silence behind your wordy
manners is deadening: a darkness that grows
like a murder of crows beating the sky
with their gallows' wings. You will hang
like any bird on fire that sings in a cloudy
noose, and your sharpened pricks
of nothing will not fly to you my friend.

THE SUICIDE DOLL

Behind my left eye is a room
with a locked door. Dry bones
and rags litter the old linoleum floor.
Sometimes a word, scent, sound, face
or flash of light unclamps the lock
and puts me there. I sit on an empty
milk crate in the room's centre,
the door closed. In the corner, the suicide
doll, wrinkled and small as a premature
baby, and blue all over like night.
With cloudy eyes it speaks to me.
It says I'm a stupid, ugly thing that can't
be loved. It tells me to burn or cut
my arms, to bruise my face, drink
until my mind goes black, drive needles
into veins to punish myself until I sleep.
It offers me peace. My lips flutter
and twitch like stuck worms on cement
as I mouth the words from memory.
The room is a deep freeze. I knead
white knuckles into arms and legs,
to make blood flow through flesh,
to make me feel. My teeth are clacking
spasms. They cut my tongue. I tell myself
the doll is a liar. I tell myself the doll
isn't real. The room is silent now.
The moon through the broken window
silvers everything. A breeze stirs
the rags and bones. They begin to move.
They rise and gather in the air; become
a dancing, human shape. I clap
my hands as it begins to sing.

AN ANGEL WITH BAD TEETH AND SMALL HANDS

An angel with bad teeth and small hands
lives beneath our back porch stairs.

Sometimes on summer nights
she sings. I'm twelve, lying in bed,
climbing my thoughts through blackness
to the moon's tunnel-mouth
into the cold silver when I hear her.

At first, it's a faint tune on a penny whistle,
then it's a voice singing words
I've never heard before. I get up,
go to the open window and look out
at our backyard, the alley
and Rachel Sullivan's house.

A wailing, sharp, the sound of diamond
slicing glass makes me bang my head
against the window frame
and bite my tongue. I yelp and spit
blood on the dirty T-shirt at my feet.

A cloud like a giant warship
passes across the moon and the stars.
I see a shape moving from the back stairs
across the yard to the alley. She's leaving,
heading toward the woods and the river.

I want to follow her, but it isn't time.
I lay back on the bed and let my mouth
fill with blood and the taste of salt.
I will find her there.

BLACK TAMBOURINE

The ocean is close tonight, the wind brings
it to us. Dead leaves drop from trees
like small pieces of darkness. I remember
a movie from my childhood: *Something Wicked
This Way Comes*. How quickly age descends on us.
Our memories are maps to places that don't exist.
I was an emperor on a green lawn wearing a white sheet
and a paper crown. The birds sang my praises
from the hedges and the trees. I dipped my tongue
into a packet of sugary crystals turning it purple.
The moon glares between two buildings like a face
between bars, a face scarred by wires. Gold tendrils
hang from the bowed heads of sunflowers lit
by street lamps at the end of this alley of backyards.
I am almost home. The ocean is so close tonight.
As I fall to sleep an old tinker shakes a black tambourine
by a pile of rags stinking of grease and gasoline.
When he opens his toothless mouth to sing,
his wine-coloured tongue flickers like a flag.

ACKNOWLEDGEMENTS

I'd like to thank Russell Thornton and Chris Hutchinson for their generous feedback on these poems in their early stages, Kate Wattie and Kali Malinka at Tonic Records for their ongoing encouragement and support, Marjorie Haynes for her love of poetry, and Amber McMillan and Silas White for helping me to become a better poet.

Rodney DeCroo is a Vancouver-based (via Pittsburgh, Pennsylvania) poet and singer-songwriter. His first collection of poetry was *Allegheny, BC*, published by Nightwood Editions in 2012. He has also released eight albums through Northern Electric Records and Tonic Records.